Let's Learn About…
OTTERS
By: Breanne Sartori

All Rights Reserved. No part of this publication may be reproduced in any form or by any means, including scanning, photocopying, or otherwise without prior written permission of the copyright holder. Copyright © 2014

Introduction

Otters are well know for being very cute and playful animals. They are also really intelligent! Otters are small mammals that live on land but spend a lot of time in the water. They are found almost all over the world and very popular in zoos.

What Otters Look Like

Otters look a lot like weasels or beavers. They are furry and small with long, think bodies and small legs. They have a small head that is dominated by their big black nose!

Fur

Otters have a very thick coat of fur – almost an inch thick. This is because they have more than one layer! There are thinner, shorter layers close to the skin which trap air to keep them warm and dry.

Feet

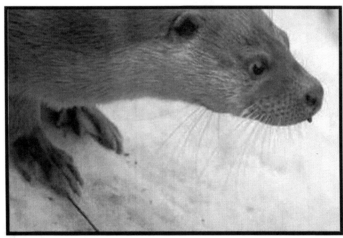

Otters have five toes on each feet that are webbed. This helps them move quickly through water. Each toe also has a sharp, strong claw. This helps them catch their prey and move easily along muddy banks.

Teeth

An adult otter has 32 teeth which includes 4 sharp canines. These canines are used to tightly hold onto their prey. Their teeth are so sharp they can even bite through shells of some animals!

Where Otters Live

Otters love freezing cold water! They can be found on every continent except Australia and Antarctica. They spend most of their time in the water but build themselves homes on land that are sometimes very far away from the water. These are called holts.

Sleeping

Sleeping otters are incredibly cute! Even though they build their homes on the land, it's not uncommon for them to sleep in the water. They will float on their backs and hold onto each other's hands to keep themselves from being separated!

Swimming

Otters are very graceful swimmers! They can only swim as fast as about 7 miles per hour, but they are very skilled so they can hunt easily. Their back feet are very good flippers and their long muscular tail helps them change direction quickly.

What Otters Eat

Otters are carnivores which means that they only eat other animals. Most of the animals are sea animals such as fish, crabs and frogs. When on land they will hunt for lizards if they need food.

Hunting

For such a small animals, otters sure do hunt a lot! They can spend about 5 hours each day, morning and night, hunting for the food to survive. Otters whiskers are very sensitive and combined with their great sense of smell, prey doesn't stand a chance!

Social Lives

Otters love to be social! They spend a lot of time playing with each other. Some species can live in groups of over 100 otters although some live alone or only in pairs. The females and males only come together when it's time to mate, even if they live in the same group!

Communication

Wow otters are loud! They love to chat, so being near a group of them is very noisy. They are very intelligent though and can recognise how each other sounds! They use clicks, whistles, growls, chirps and they even chuckle to communicate with each other.

Baby Otters

Baby otters can be very hungry. They can spend up to eight hours a day feeding from their mother! They can be born both on land in their den or in the water on a floating bed! Pups are blind at birth and don't open their eyes until they are a month old.

Breeding

Otters can breed at any time of the year – it depends when the males decide to go looking for the females! They can have up to six pups in a litter, but usually only have one. Otters can start breeding again as soon as they give birth, but they usually wait until about a year so that they can look after their young.

The Life of an Otter

Otters grow quickly and no longer need to feed from their mother at about 12 months old. They don't start breeding until they are two or three though. Otters can live to be 15 years old, but it is very dangerous when they are a pup. Only a third of pups survive their first year.

Predators

Poor otters have predators on the land *and* in the water. On land they need to watch out for coyotes and eagles, especially young otters. Sharks, sea lions and killer whales prey on them in the water.

Other Dangers

Unfortunately humans are the most dangerous animal for otters. Humans kill them for their fur or to protect their fishing spots. Otters can also die from starvation if their teeth wear out. If they eat a lot of shells and break their teeth, they aren't able to catch prey anymore.

Protecting Themselves

Otters have some weapons at their disposal but they aren't really a match for their predators. Their tail is very muscular and can be used to hit predators. Their teeth and claws also act as weapons!

Sea Otter

The Sea Otter is the heaviest of all otters, but with it's small round face it's possibly the cutest too! They live in the north of the Pacific Ocean and many choose to live around California. Some Sea Otters have purple teeth because of all the purple sea urchins they eat!

Giant Otter

The giant otter is a very different size and shape to other otter species, so many people think it's another animal altogether! They are found in fresh water rivers and streams throughout South America. They are very social and are always found in huge groups.

Northern River Otter

Northern River Otters are very long with big heads, lots of fur and long whiskers. They are found along rivers in Canada and the United States. They don't spend as much time on land as other otters and even dig under-water burrows to their dens!

Made in the USA
Lexington, KY
05 February 2018